WINDOW AND MIRROR

POETRY BY
TED VIRTS

atmosphere press

© 2024 Ted Virts

Published by Atmosphere Press

Cover design by Ronaldo Alves

No part of this book may be reproduced without permission from the author except in brief quotations and in reviews.

Atmospherepress.com

In memory of my dad, Sam Virts,
who taught me how to love language.

In deep gratitude to my life companion, Charlene Virts,
who has spent decades teaching me what love means.

One of the source words for the word "dedication" means to "declare solemnly." These two taught me with such fun and frolic that "solemn" isn't quite accurate. I'll just say that without their presence, my life would be severely impoverished.

ABOUT THE COVER

Henri Mattisse (1869-1954). *Entrance to the Kasbah*. 1912. A Kasbah is a fortress, a guarded royal palace, or protected residence. To enter a Kasbah is to see what is hidden and valued—a glimpse into a private life.

PRAISE FOR *WINDOW* AND *MIRROR*

"Colorful and precise descriptions and interesting formatting take readers into Virts' world. He demonstrates humanity: We are all bound by similar experiences, vulnerabilities, and strengths. This is a free verse feast for the mind and soul that you will want to read more than once."

- Cammy Marble, author of *Holiday In the Trees* series

"Ted Virts' *Window and Mirror* is an unassuming collection which forthrightly encourages the reader to look, to listen, and in so doing, to come home to oneself. These poems tackle the grand questions that have propelled us since the advent of human life, but the answers given are simple ones, shaped by unplanned conversations, and by the vivid presence of iris, cactus, mesquite, quail and chickadees. The unifying theme of the collection is apparent not only in the title, but in the author's introduction to the text, and in what he shares about his life in the bio. So many poignant poems here stop me in my tracks, inviting me to be deeply present with what is offered, and to carry that invitation to situations I contend with beyond the author's reach.

One of my favorites is a poem titled "Park Bench" in which we encounter Jesus. When we assume the poet's persona and summon our courage to ask a troubling question, he replies "I love these fall colors." This unapologetic acceptance informs the work throughout. In the stunning poem "Soup Cans from My Dad," the lessons from father to child become even more vivid after his passing. In "My Brother Comes Home," the poet recalls his baby brother "isn't much bigger than/ the football I want to throw to him." In the dual meaning of window as mirror, the poet's outward gaze yields inward resonance, deliberately aided by metaphor. In the hands that work clay, we are "Broken free." In a poem for a friend on the death of her husband, we find "We are old/ We know/ the slow dance of joy and sadness together". One poem urges us to "sit" four times. Indeed, these are poems which invoke all that is possible in the stillness, lifting even simple acts to the resilience of being "crowned/crossed/blessed".

- Carol Barrett, Ph.D., author of *Reading Wind* and *Pansies*

"The thirst for life, the awe of the present, spoken in Latin in search of the holy, Ted's book *Window and Mirror* examines the reflection of self through the view of the world from the kitchen table, heartfelt and authentic. Be still and Know... I invite you to meditate and reflect with Ted through triumph, faith, doubt, and everything that that life brings. Upon reading *Window and Mirror* you will find a community with the knowledge we are not alone."

- Andrew Cloninger, author of *C6-C7*

"Ted Virts has a style that seamlessly presents the past/present divide as a continuum of poignant memory and hopeful being. His poems echo sacred knowledge, passed down through living and loving, despite the loss and pain. Both religion and secularism are presented as equally sacred, their rituals recorded in an unassuming manner that the reader can easily discern. The incomplete past frames the fearful future, reminding us that hope is always there, waiting for us to discover, if we take time to look. Great poetry!"

- Jerry Lovelady,
author of *The Weight of Our Wishes: Poems for a new Humanity*.

"Ted Virts' poetry in *Window and Mirror* intersects his mindful philosophy with vivid settings, reflective emotion and powerful imagery. Use of crafted details become microcosms of our daily struggles, while his poems return to us again and again as long-lost friends who carry the truth. A must-read, you will find simple gifts on each page that remind you of your everyday treasures in your life."

- Linda Fifer, author of
The Road Between Two Skies, *Finding the Grain* and *Winter's Turn*

"Throughout his poetry collection *Window and Mirror*, Ted Virts draws the reader into a reflective state with a series of questions—big questions about love, about faith, about meaning. The poet nods to Descartes—*I think therefore I am*—omitting the oft-ignored beginning of the quote, "*I doubt*, therefore I think therefore I am," and yet this sacred doubt infuses the verse with an authenticity of emotion that threads from ocean to desert, and through time itself. The poet is pilgrim, underwater, thirsty in the desert (*this is my cactus life*), viscerally aware of others who thirst. In these poems, a father quells the ersatz-Toastmaster nerves of his children by having them clutch soup cans as they narrate their stories; light is a marker of time and of return (*lights on a house / lights on a cake*). In "Park Bench," the inquisitive speaker takes a seat next to Jesus. Does he get answers? In these poems, the living is in the questioning: *Life is a prayer*, and perhaps prayer is but a sacred question. *I remember joy*, says the poet: answer, and beauty, enough."

- Irene Cooper,
author of *spare change* and *even my dreams are over the constant state of anxiety*

"Through *Window and Mirror* we view a world Ted Virts sculpts in poetic verse, an exploration and exultation of the miracles in what we see, do, and think on a daily basis. Bringing us through presence and absence, desert and ocean, pilgrims passing through temptation, saints carrying aching souls, a sister's dying husband, and grief for a rift between two brothers, Ted allows us to stop and realize that 'everyone is right in a way'. Come to 'this room / this place / this moment', where 'Your life is prayer' and you are 'Broken free.'"

- Julie S. Paschold, author of *Horizons* (2024 Nebraska Book Award winner), *You Have Always Been Here*, and *Human Nature*.

Contents

Introduction	1
Presence/Absence	2
Write an "I Am" Poem	4
Introibo	6
Ocotillo	8
Beginnings	9
Story Time	11
Text in the Time of Politics	12
Pandemics	13
Thoughts about Jesus: Yarn	14
Rainbow	15
Small Town	16
My Sister Calls	18
To Choose a Kettle Bell	19
Soup Cans from My Dad	20
My Brother Comes Home	22
Park Bench	23
Eve's Eyes	24
Frame of Departure	25
Obvious Thief	26
Clay Breaks Free	28
Seer	29
December	30
Sacred Acts	31
Slow Dance	32
Near the Border	34
Sonora	35
Decades	38
To Sit	39
Downstream	40
The Obstetrician of Iris	41
Christmas Artichoke	42

Introduction

What are we doing here? I look out at a congregation. I watch birds in my backyard. I note rite and ritual in everyday life. What are we doing? What do we notice about this place, this time? These poems are snapshots of what I notice about the life I am living and the world I am observing. There is a sacredness to everyday life—profound and silly, sad and hopeful, woeful and wonderful. Drama takes place in the stories we tell and hear of the day's anecdotes, the TV and news, the decisions and results, plans and folly. Those stories are the stuff of literature, music, theater and more.

Telling and hearing form the basis of my life and career. The struggles of families to make a life and a living are framed in question, celebration, frustration, and fun. What can I do now? How could that have happened to me? It isn't fair! She did well! I'm so proud. What does a god want from me? Was it meant to be? It is my fault. It is their fault. How will I live now that death has taken him? Why is she like that?

We live in a galaxy with millions of stars, among billions of galaxies. Do we matter? What am I supposed to do? Who am I supposed to be? What does a god do for me? Am I loved? Do I belong? Why all the world's suffering? Why my own suffering?

The poems here thread their way through my life's questions, the people and events that I have been able to see, to remember and to value. The silly and serious, the petty and profound all have a place. Life is mystery. Life is prayer.

Presence/Absence

    Ocean
Self-Contained Underwater
Breathing Apparatus

A full air tank can last
more than an hour
at twenty feet under water

  Sit.
before a coral head
breathe slowly wait

life comes forth
to see you
to be seen:
    Christmas tree worms peek from coral heads
    reef fish lurch
      to defend their eggs
    even the octopus
      betrays her rock-like
      camouflage

    Desert
The canteen is
  required here
Do not begin your hike
  if the air is
  above 110 degrees

Boots scrunch
  sand, rock, powder
Spine, needles, nettles, thorns
  reach for skin and clothing
aggressive stance
  for protection

  Sit.
  Crouch before the land

life comes forth
    to see you
    to be seen:
        Birds caw
        lizards move
        quail scurry from shade to shade
        ants, scorpions
            go about their business

Night

Light leaves
dark arises
    Sit.   Be still.

In the sea   some fish spin cocoons
        for a night's safety
        some,
        in trance-like stillness,
        glide motionless
        lest they be seen
            the hunters begin their work
            seeing what others do not

In the desert   a cactus releases stored air
        javelinas call
        coyotes gather
        life comes forth
        in the cool dark

The Soul's Dark Night

The presence of the holy
    feels absent
certainty is
clothed in doubt
what is present
is absence

Sit.   Breathe.   Wait.

Write an "I Am" Poem

Descartes says, "I think therefore I am."

I am thinking
        about what I'm thinking about

I am thinking about
   who I am
I am what I am
   —God and Popeye the Sailor Man
   make that claim

Am I a self?
Am I a true self?
Am I a false self?

Do I have a self
   or am I one?
Do I have a thought
   or am I one?
Am I many selves
   or am I One?

I am a complex machine
I am unsure how it works
I am unsure how to use it

I am an old man
I am not as young as
   I used to be
     Even a second ago
     I was younger

I am confused
I am fused
I am refused

I am overused
I am underused
I am used

I am used to it
    of course
    off course
    sometimes coarse
    sometimes not

I am held
I am held together
I am trying not to fall apart

I have a heart
I have a love
I have a joy
I have a fear

I am not my heart
I am not my love
I am not my joy
I am not my fear

I am
I am not
I have
I have not
I wonder
I wander

I am therefore
    —I think

Introibo

Introibo ad altare Dei
"I will go unto the altar of God,"
the priest said.
Ad Deum qui laetificat juventutem meam
"To God who gives joy to my youth,"
I responded. I wore my altar boy's black cassock.
The Mass began.

I stand in Mexico today, decades later,
sixty miles from the US border.
I peer down through glass at bones of beloved Padre Kino.
A black cassocked Jesuit,
three centuries ago he knew God among ancient tribes:
Pima, Yaqui, Tohono O'odham.

Above the bones,
in the church of Magdalena de Kino,
a wooden statue of the good padre's patron saint,
Saint Francis Xavier,
lies in rest.

Pilgrims travel to this place.
They pass through the stark mystery of the Sonoran desert—
some from Arizona's Tubac, some from neighboring villages—
San Ignacio, Imuris, Santa Ana.

Revelers—pilgrims of a different sort—encircle the church
to dance, to drink, to sing, to shout.

Pilgrims pass through this temptation.
They approach the shrine.
They circle the freshly painted, pink-faced saint's form.
Men—hats carried.
Women—heads covered.

Teary eyed,
one after the other,
they bend to kiss the saint's forehead.
Hand beneath the carved form,
they tenderly lift the saint's silent likeness.

> *Cancer took my brother, I am lost.*
> *My mother can't remember my name.*
> *My husband tells me I am not enough.*
> *My little girl cries. She doesn't want to live.*
> *My little boy has no friends.*
> *I am alone.*
> *I am afraid.*

Lifting sadness and fear,
they cross themselves in ancient, hopeful ritual.
The saint carries the heart's ache.
God might see, heal,
touch and lift them.

Long past youth
I join the procession
I approach the altar of God
I remember joy
I remember temptation

I touch the saint
I lift his wooden form
I ask for joy,
once again,
to lift my wooden heart.

Ocotillo

The pale, spiked wood looks dead
    spines and thorns, evolved from leaves and branches,
    left behind weaponry
    guards this abandoned fortress
Today though
    fragile green
    leaves emerge, reaching up
    within the greyed sticks
Sharp, unmoved spears
    form a haven against
    javelina hunger

This is my cactus life

A craving
    to be seen
    to be touched
    to feel the warm caress of quiet
        that lures green life
        up from thorns
        of noise and worry

Beginnings

Inuit:
    There was a time
    when time hadn't yet been dreamed
    a stone and soil fell through sky
        babies emerged from the land
        like flowers
    each creature understood the other

Shoshoni:
    Babies fell
    from a sacred jar
    that watered the land
    Trumpeter Swan brought
    peace to tribe, deer and fish

Yaqui:
    Before the knowing of planting
    animals and turtles lived
    on land and water
    one tree linked land and sky
    giving visions of how animals and people can live

Floods and fears
        Hopes and heroes
                Gods and Grace

Catechism:
    Adam and Eve
    walk with God
    taste Good and Evil
        and are cast out of the garden

Sunday School:
    Felt-board shapes
    a flood
    an angry God starts over

Sermon:
    There was one language
    confounded
    lest humans become God-like

Every night's newscast:
        floods
        fires
        heat
        dust
        famine
        fear

Too distracted to dream
    too vain for visions
        too afraid for peace

        our ending begins

Story Time

    "Good evening."
Amna and Geoff enter my living room through my TV set.
I hear their stories every night.
With horror, humor and hope
they engross me with today's tales.
    Heat, famine
    Conflicts, cruelty
    Palace intrigue among princes and politicians
    Sadness and sorrow
    Ignorance and arrogance
    People, power, and policy collide.

Each night the stories repeat.
    Characters snarling, weeping, raging.

Amna says, "In other news..."
    A soccer team sings hope.
    A poet pleads for presence.
    An artist sees beauty amidst burden.

Geoff says, "Thanks for spending part of your evening with us."

Contradictions and complexity.
I turn off the TV set.
I stare at the dark screen.
Dinner awaits.

Text in the Time of Politics

Every two hours
Joe Biden sends me a note.
Adam Schiff, Hillary, Barack, and Kamala
all remember me and send a note too.
I am important!
Joe writes,
    "Can I ask you to spare three dollars?"
Joe says it will save
    the economy
    the right to vote
    the nation
    the climate
Joe asks,
    Do I want everyone to have healthcare?
    Do I think responsible gun laws are important?
    Should corruption be banished?
    How about a balanced judiciary?
    How about a realistic minimum wage?
    How about a fair tax law?
I say,
    Yes! Yes! Yes! And I want more.
      Better wages for teachers!
      Fair immigration practice!
      Let's make it so that kids have lunch,
        even when schools are closed!
      How about keeping the police from killing black people!
And, Joe, while you are at it,
    could we bring the civil back to our discourse?
Here's $3.00.   I'm counting on you!

Pandemics

> "The US has a silent pig pandemic at its door once again."
> *The Guardian* 10/17/21

The warning came yesterday:
        a silent pig pandemic at our door...again

We didn't answer last time—
        Did we not hear?

Wilber has no word for his friend Charlotte and her web
There are no squeals of delight
There is no objection to porcine body shaming
They pig out in monastic meditation
Mud baths are silent

The march to market is stoic
Many morosely remain home
They just eat their roast beef
Or, tongue tied, have none
No cries of "wee, wee, wee"

Quiet cringing to the wolf's huffing and puffing
No pronouncements from the poke

They are smart, no doubt
Voluntarily drinking to excess,
        unable to comment to their drinking buddies
            human or snouted
They only gesture at their truffle finds
We bring home the bacon
        They have nothing to say

Thoughts about Jesus: Yarn

likes to stick to itself.
There can be an afternoon
spent
unraveling
untangling
looking to find a single strand through the jumble.

A weaver takes a skein.
With the help of a rotating frame
      (a niddy noddy—fun to say)
she begins
trying to tame the apparently logical skein
into a ball—easy to hold
          less likely to knot up.

Too often an impossible mess is the Gordian result.

Is there a strand to find you, Jesus?

The stories stick together. They defy pulling apart.

I tug on one string
          once I was lost; now I am found

I pull another
          no one goes to the Father without me

a knot appears
          am I loved? am I on trial?

To look up is to see
      billions of stars
To look down is to see
      my meager decades of living
I look to you
      an afternoon spent.

Rainbow

Never again will I strike down every living thing as I have done...
When I bring clouds over the earth and the bow is seen in the clouds...
I will remember my covenant that is between me and you and every living creature...
the waters shall never again become a flood to destroy all flesh.
Genesis 8-9

My little girl asks,
"Look! Daddy!
Colors in the sky!
What is that?"

Promise
Regret
Apology

Small Town

You look out from the car window.
The hours pass, filled with green-blue sagebrush.
You ride with me from your mom's.
A week with dad.

You are ten.
You sit on the grass.
The big birch shades the July heat.
I see you through the living room shades.

You walk around the town.
The Nevada wind blows weeds and sand
across your skinny legs.
Will you find friends?
I watch you and worry.

Then the parade starts.
    The flags
    The star-spangled kids on bikes
    The ambulance
    The firetruck
You ride in the front seat
like you belong there.

The random siren splits the silence.
A Fourth of July necessity.
You circle the small town twice.
You grin.

Later in the week, your bike hits a car.
I'm scared.
They tell me right away.
You are OK. It is a small town.
You rest on the front lawn,
leaning against the big birch tree.
I watch behind the living room shades.
How will the visit be?

My Sister Calls

White-crowned sparrows
visit in the spring
They scratch the ground
both frantic feet at once

They look for food
tolerate each other
fight sometimes
rapidly over-running the yard
over-looking the obvious

My sister calls to ask about prayer
Her husband is dying
> Her friends tell her,
>> "God will heal him if God wants to"
> Her friends tell her,
>> "God might take you first"
> I offer,
>> What is prayer to the anxious sparrow
>>> scratching out a living?
>> Your life is prayer
>> If you slow down
>> God will meet you

To Choose a Kettlebell

It should be too heavy
to hold
straight out
with both arms

Russians used them
to weigh grain

The trick is the swing
do not lift—
pendulum
        pelvic thrust
                back straight
        don't squat
let the weight work

back and forth
        back and forth
        maybe for an instant
let it balance

hold it still if you can
        the weight
                falls again
        keeping time

the grandfather clock
                back and forth
        swings on its own
weight

you try to hold it
it falls again
another year passes

Soup Cans from My Dad

We were five
        squirmy siblings.
Me, the oldest,
        the three sisters,
                my toddler brother.

You   would line us up.
               Each of us took a turn
               to stand in front of the fireplace.

You   would suggest the topic:
               a favorite dinner,
               an animal to be,
               a bike.

You   would caution
               Don't say "um."
               Tell me more.

One   at a time
               we would stand
               to speak
               holding soup cans
               in our hands
               so as not to touch our faces.

We   would stammer stories.
You   would grin with delight.

Five years ago,
one at a time,
we stood again to stammer our stories
in front of your photo,
gripping the podium
       like soup cans,
trying not to say "um"
through glistening eyes.

My Brother Comes Home

With the world view of an eight-year-old,
I am the center of the universe.
My sisters are a mere inconvenience.
But then my mom says I am going
to have a brother.
That will be fun, I think.
Someone to play catch.
Someone different from the girls in the house.

The day comes,
but he isn't much bigger than
the football I want to throw to him.

We fight sometimes.
We have skinny arms.
We wear blue jeans and white tee shirts.
We have blonde crew cuts and black tennis shoes.

He starts high school
at the same yellow-halled prep school I attended,
the same starched button-down shirt,
the same khaki pants.
The teachers ask him, "Aren't you Ted's brother?"

I finish college.
I study psychology and theology.
Everyone is right in a way.

He's an engineer.
You are right or you are wrong.

We both want to be right.
We never play catch.

Park Bench

Jesus sits on the park bench.
He looks at fall colors,
        splendid this year,
and feels at one with the universe.
He does that a lot.

I walk up.

"Can I join you?"
        "Sure, of course," he says.
"What should I call you?"
        "'J' is just fine, " he says.
"That's my brother's name."
        "I know," he says.

I sit. I say,
"Do you mind a few questions?"
        "If you must. I don't mind. Really."
"Thanks.
        I'm not sure of what to think about you.
                Son of God?
                Judge of heaven and earth?
                Wizard?
                Brother?
                Friend?"
        "Just call me 'J'," he says.

"So, what am I to do?
        Worship?
        Keep kosher?
        Kill the infidel?
        Hope things are OK now
                between your dad and us?
        I'm confused," I say.
Jesus looks at me.
He says,
        "I love these fall colors."

Eve's Eyes

> *"God knows when you eat of it your eyes will be opened and you will be like God, knowing good and evil"...When the woman saw that the tree was a delight to the eyes and that the tree was to be desired to make one wise, she took the fruit and ate it.*
> Genesis 3

How much more can eyes be opened?

The fruit—luminous

I want to see
       to touch
       to taste
       to share
            with him

Is it to be a god
       this knowing
       this good
       this evil
            or is it to be alive?

without opened eyes
       I am blinded
without choice
       am I living?

So
       I choose
       I share
       I live

Frame of Departure

I was not big
        enough to tell you
        it is over
I become smaller
        each cliché a word meld—

It's me not you let's be friends I feel bad you deserve better

I write it down
you hold the words and look
        away
I leave, fear-filled

that your grief
would flatten
me like a bug

fear that I'd be framed
trapped in a picture of this moment
tread-milled memory
holds me in place

Shrinking from you
I strain toward another view

The image remains
       mid-sleep
       your face fills
            the familiar frame
       asking what
       even now
            I cannot answer

Obvious Thief

The army of skittish
quail wakes us
at dawn

They
eat
walk
run for the fence
their flight is
a flap of noise toward the trees
in the neighbor's yard

Chickadees
black and white
the size of a shot glass
visit as seasons
change
a stop
at the feeder
grab a bite
then fly for cover

such obvious thieves

In anonymous crowds
at the grocery
at the bar
I eat
I walk
I run from small talk
and neighbor courtesies

Hello
at the mailbox
Nod
on the street
Wave
through a car window

I watch
teens slump to school
then return home

I enjoy their games
their chatter
Me—
such an obvious thief

Clay Breaks Free

Genesis says
humans are the clay
the humus
not in the clay
just clay.

Then the divine hand starts to play—
shapes—snakes and balls (every preschooler knows)
stick together.

Divine breath—
then living beings break forth
break free
to see each other
to see the divine hand.

It doesn't go so well.
Lunch at the tree of knowledge
ends badly.

Yet we are set free.
Broken free.

Seer

Once the birdsong quiets down
the tour begins
Coffee in hand
slippered feet
she forgets the garden shoes

> I follow along
> I look at yesterday's plants
> I notice a new color
> a flower, a leaf recently arrived

She sees

> This (unpronounceable) plant
> is breaking through
> The bud is about out
> This one is not doing so well

>> I marvel
>> at what her world might
>> be like

She sees
> a thread she dropped in a weaving
> a plant too large
> a color just right
> or a yarn too thin

>> I follow along
>>> I see only her.

December

Across the street
all day
the neighbor has planned
the lights
to frame his house

While walking on the roof
to light the eves
it is cold enough for a hat
cold enough for a jacket

December
no snow yet

Some have studded their tires
some drive slower

Happy birthday wishes land on my computer
offers of discount dinners—after I buy one—
to help me celebrate

The lights come on
lights on a house
lights on a cake

Sacred Acts

a bicycle ride begins
        holy placing of a crown atop the head
                that the world might stay in balance

a car drive starts
        with crossing of the chest
                that survival will accompany the unexpected

a flight begins
        a young woman performs a two-handed
        blessing toward the exits
                so terrifying that most bow their heads
                lest the terrible reality become visible

movement begins
        crowned
        crossed
        blessed

prayer

Slow Dance

The cold outside
stings
I cross the parking lot
I wait in line
I sign the book
I take the folded piece of heavy paper
I find a place to sit

In the pew,
the face on the paper
stares at me
      His name
        two dates below the picture
The face is kind
interested
interesting

I'm here for my friend
She spent years of her life
beside this man I did not know

The room fills—a hum of quiet conversation
Star-like lights reflect on the sanctuary wall
The organist plays Beethoven
We are old
We know
the slow dance of joy and sadness together

A white-haired wife
sits close to her man
Her hand moves easily on his shoulder

Kneeling deep in prayer a woman looks up,
makes a place for another
A greeting, a concerned smile

The music changes
Escorted, cane in hand,
my friend makes her way to the front row

Speakers
        pray/talk/remember
Words drift like a familiar song
        Celebration / Good Life / Hope / Good Death
        Years / Travels / Seasons / Stories

Can she listen?

She looks at the photograph
What does she see?
        a touch of a hand
        a shared laugh
        a worry
        a tear
        a last kiss

We stand
then sing
Joyful, Joyful
We sing
Let All Things Now Living

We shuffle out—
        ...all things now living
She leads the way
a cane
a slow walk

Church coffee in hand,
I wonder what muffled phrase to offer

I share what I can
I cross the cold parking lot

Near the Border

Forty feet across, ragged arms drifting green
        scratch a half-circle in sky.

From within the Mesquite
        a hundred-mouthed, multi-toned song
            moves above the small brick porch,
                cacophony of call and caw.

Mesquite and me in mirrored stare
        our years—similar
        our limbs—soft-leafed invitation,
                sharp-thorned protection.

Curved-bill Thrasher, Townsend's Warbler
        huit and chirp.
Black-Throated Sparrow, White-Winged Dove
        sing and hoot.
Wind, a whispered roar.
Tree song.
Setting sun.

Sonora

                                                               Listen!
                                                              Arroyo
                                                      the sound
                      whispers gentle across the tongue
                              a breeze moves leaves
                                       a quiet ballet
Truck tires crunch,
the gravel wash climbs the canyon.
                    "They most likely walked this way,
                    stumbling across rocks
                    bound for Baboquivari
                    Tohono O'odham sacred mountain
                    where the coyotes pointed."
                                                  Listen!
                                             Caliente
                                       the sound
                        clicks from the jaw and tongue
                              chewing the word
                                    a bird song
                          cascading from cactus
The desert guards itself
spikes protect plants
lizards lie below branches
heat waves wrinkle the view.
                    "If they were able,
                    they found mesquite tree shade and
                    hopes of a breeze to cool sweat-soaked shirts."
                                                   Listen!
                                              Aqua
                               the parched sound
                              catches in the neck
                              a hard stop then
                                the exhale ends

A look east
A blue flag
rises
above the water barrel.
    "They found the flag
    and the now-empty bullet-riven hope.
    They left slowly,
    despair
    as dusty as the endless walk ahead."
              Listen!
              Ayúdame
           escapes the lungs
         like a last breath precedes
            a death rattle
   "The group split up.
   See the steps. Carpet strapped on shoes
   to mask the marks in the sand.
   Younger and stronger went ahead.
   The woman, child heavy, waits."
Desert heat is pushed out
as night chills the land.
She lies still. No longer feeling the ground.
The next day she is found.
              Listen!
              Las Cruces
           bounces in the ear
     the sound made with a kiss-shaped mouth
           ending with cheeks lifted
             a slight grin
We come to the cross
one of a thousand
cascading across this cactus crowded country.
A crumpled proclamation is lifted from a container
to tell of the corpse of the mother to be.

In silence we stand.
We find a nearby stone
place it on the cross piece
in sad remembrance
of this mother we never knew.

We leave without a sound.

Decades

Mom confides in me—
    Dad drinks too much
    they fight
        I am ten

I remember him singing
    "Born to Lose"

My dad and I drive to my apartment
    he has a bottle of port
    we share it
        I am twenty
    he is talking about his life
    it was decades ago

I visit him in Lodi
    my mom died a few months ago
    he listens to classical music
    it is loud enough he can't hear me knock
        She was seventy
        I am forty

In memory care he asks for sherry
    I won't buy it for him
        I am sixty

He died in his nineties
I am seventy
I prefer whiskey
though tonight, the sherry is good enough

To Sit

        clear air hovers
        night floats down

        my little world
              neither good
              nor bad

what is
    is

this room
    this time
        this place
        rests amid
   stars
       galaxies

    I belong

what is
    is

this room
    this place
        this moment

Downstream

He knows me when I see him
though today I have become his brother
in childhood pranks

He still likes women
though he forgets their names
they become lovers
with changed faces
he still reaches out to touch them

It is not so bad
being in his mind's long-life story
except that I didn't show up
until he was twenty-five

There was a time when I would call
he would answer his phone
numbers and machines are now lost in fog
he would listen
he would let go of his worries

Now time is like air
no edges
no lines
he is grateful and gracious nonetheless
he remembers that some things
can end
he's just not sure how

My dad has gone downstream
I follow
sometimes close

Lately I can't catch up

The Obstetrician of Iris

Each morning
eager leaves stand
reaching for touch

when the light is right
              she approaches
    sensing
    assessing the promise
she offers
    a tender touch
    a kind caress
    a soft sigh

each day
hope-full
waiting
repeats

Until

the light is right
the blossom
the delight

Christmas Artichoke

As Christmas approaches
Some see the town get warm and kind, generous and happy.
Most of the time, I agree.

Christmas is an artichoke.
It takes work to enjoy it.
You have to pull away the leaves.
The leaves resist, of course.
Enjoy a small taste,
but you must leave the leaves aside.
They are not the point. They are in the way.

Say goodbye to each leaf.
Don't worry—
> the herald angels will still sing,
> the manger will still be warmed by the animals' steady breathing,
> shepherds will still go to see the thing that has taken place,

just set them aside for a while.
> Don't forget the trimmed trees,
> the stockings hung by the chimney with care,
> the packages and tinsel, and, yes,
> kneeling Santa. They will all survive.

For some, set aside pointers and reminders of something more.
For others, set aside things that are distasteful and just hard to swallow.

When you have pulled away enough, you might get a glimpse:
Christmas, at its best, is not just a special time.
It is a return home to who you are at heart.

Acknowledgments

My wonderful ideas and images always seem great in my head. Then I write them down and realize I need some help. With gratitude, I want to give a deeply felt nod of appreciation to a number of folks:

Writing down the Baja—a week long workshop and experience in Todos Santos, Baja Sur, Mexico. Convener Ellen Waterston's wit, wisdom and delightful insight returned me to focused writing. Ellen was named Poet Laureate of Oregon in August, 2024.

The Forge, Bend, Oregon—a ten-month journey of zoom, writing and more, led me to greater depth of what I was doing and trying to do. Mike Cooper, Irene Cooper and Ellen Santasiero provided differing approaches to expanding and improving how to think and practice my efforts.

Carol Barrett, who invited me into *Porch Poets*, a monthly small group of Bend writers, and Irene Cooper, both pointed toward ways to improve this manuscript.

It goes without saying that the chemistry, comments and collegiality of my fellow writers helped me immeasurably.

My first and primary reader is my wife. Throughout our four decades of friendship and marriage, she has listened, suggested and reminded me that people appreciate what I say and write, even when I wasn't so sure.

Some of the works here have appeared in the following anthologies:

Sonora was an honorable mention in *Verseweavers: the Oregon Poetry Association Anthology of Prize-Winning Poems*, Number 28, 2023.

Baja Benediction, 2022, included earlier versions of "Soup Cans from My Dad," "Frame of Departure," and "Presence/Absence."

Central Oregon Writer's Guild Literary Collection, 2022, included "Obstetrician of Iris," "Pandemics", and" Park Bench." The COWG Literary Collection of 2023 included an earlier version of "Near the Border" under the title of "Mesquite Melody."

About Atmosphere Press

Founded in 2015, Atmosphere Press was built on the principles of Honesty, Transparency, Professionalism, Kindness, and Making Your Book Awesome. As an ethical and author-friendly hybrid press, we stay true to that founding mission today.

If you're a reader, enter our giveaway for a free book here:

SCAN TO ENTER
BOOK GIVEAWAY

If you're a writer, submit your manuscript for consideration here:

SCAN TO SUBMIT
MANUSCRIPT

And always feel free to visit Atmosphere Press and our authors online at atmospherepress.com. See you there soon!

About the Author

TED VIRTS' life has wandered and wondered through preschool teaching, labor in startup manufacturing, Planned Parenthood management, ministry and pastoral supervision. There were stops along the way: Korea, the Philippines, China, the Caribbean, Mexico and the Arctic. There were stumbles and sorrows, play and puzzles: SCUBA diving, triathlons, friends lost and found, dulcimer playing, academic degrees, divorces, a happy marriage of forty-two years to Charlene, and homes in desert, suburbia and forests of the Western US. Ted and Charlene are recent residents of southern Arizona.

Throughout the years, Ted has pondered what is sacred and how myth, memory, and stories from human cultures describe life and consciousness. His conclusions? The Holy surrounds us. Our task is to pause enough to notice and appreciate—then to engage enough to offer kindness, comfort, support and celebration to the world in which we belong.

www.ingramcontent.com/pod-product-compliance
Lightning Source LLC
LaVergne TN
LVHW041637070526
838199LV00052B/3411